Transport Around the World

Boats and Ships

Chris Oxlade

Heinemann
LIBRARY

www.heinemann.co.uk
Visit our website to find out more information about Heinemann Library books.

To order:
 Phone 44 (0) 1865 888066
 Send a fax to 44 (0) 1865 314091
Visit the Heinemann Bookshop at www.heinemann.co.uk to browse our catalogue
and order online.

First published in Great Britain by Heinemann Library,
Halley Court, Jordan Hill, Oxford OX2 8EJ, part of Harcourt Education.
Heinemann is a registered trademark of Harcourt Education Ltd.

Editorial: Diyan Leake and Kristen Truhlar
Design: Kimberley R. Miracle and Ray Hendren
Picture research: Erica Martin
Production: Julie Carter

Originated by Chroma Graphics (Overseas) Pte Ltd
Printed and bound in China by South China Printing Co. Ltd

ISBN 978 0 4310 8695 8

12 11 10 09 08
10 9 8 7 6 5 4 3 2 1

British Library Cataloguing in Publication Data
Oxlade, Chris
Transport Around the World: Boats and Ships

A full catalogue record for this book is available from the British
Library.

Acknowledgements
The publishers would like to thank the following for permission to
reproduce photographs: Alamy/f1 online p. **17**; Art Archive/Viking Ship
Museum Oslo/Dagli Orti p. **8**; Corbis pp. **5** (Neil Rabinowitz), **6** (Joel W.
Rogers), **9** (Joel W. Rogers), **14** (Dave G. Hauser), **16** (Dave G. Hauser),
19 (Carl Purcell), **29** (Carl Purcell); Corbis p. **28** (Zefa/Sergio Pitamitz);
Quadrant pp. **4** (Graham Laughton), **20** (Mike Nicolson), **21** (Mike
Nicolson); Rex Features p. **12** (Alex Segre); The Stock Market p. **13** (Tom
Stewart); Phil Thomas p. **8**; Tony Stone Images pp. **10** (Gordon Fisher),
11 (Tony Craddock), **22** (Vince Streano), **23** (Sylvain Grandadam), **24**
(John Lund), **25** (Ian Murphy), **26** (Oli Tennant), **27** (James Bareham);
Trip pp. **15** (M. Garrett), **18** (H. Rogers).

The publishers would like to thank Carrie Reiling for her assistance in the
publication of this book.

Cover photograph of a tall ship reproduced with permission of
Getty Images (Greg Pease).

Contents

Some words are shown in bold, **like this**. You can find out what they mean by looking in the glossary.

What is a boat?

A boat is a small craft that floats on water. People use boats for fishing, for travelling and for fun. Ships are bigger than boats. They are mainly used for transport.

sail

Families can have fun on small sailboats like this.

A captain needs charts to know which way to go.

All ships have a **crew** of sailors. They **steer** the ship and work its machinery. The captain is the person in charge of the ship and its crew.

How boats work

Some small boats are moved along with paddles. A kayak needs a paddle to make it go forward. The paddler also uses the paddle to **steer** to the left or right.

paddler

paddle

Kayaks can be used on lakes and rivers.

Larger boats and ships have an **engine** that turns a **propeller**. The propeller pushes the boat through the water. A **rudder** steers the boat to the left or to the right.

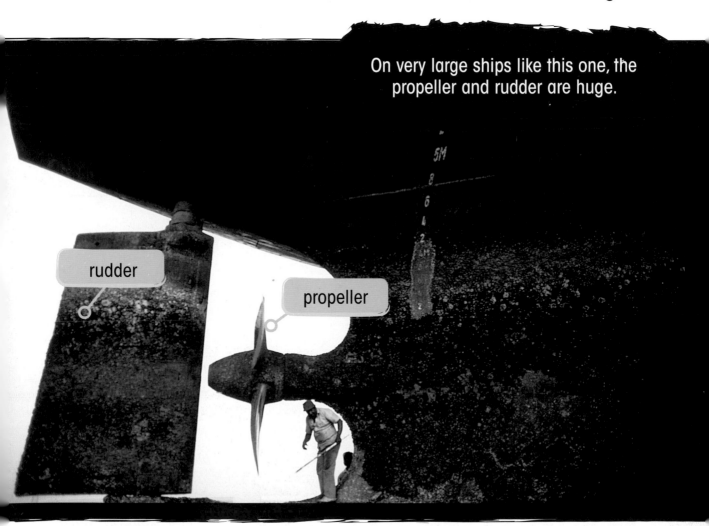

On very large ships like this one, the propeller and rudder are huge.

rudder

propeller

The first boats

People built long wooden boats about a thousand years ago. Longboats had oars to make them go. Some longboats also had a square sail.

The people who built longboats like this one were called Vikings.

Ships used to be the only way to travel between continents. For a long time, people travelled on sailing ships. Steamships were first built about 170 years ago.

This steamship was called *Leviathan*. Its name means "large and powerful".

Where boats are used

Ships and large boats travel across the sea. They stop at places called **ports**. They often have to sail through stormy weather and large waves.

Ships that travel on the sea often carry lots of **cargo**.

cargo

Some boats do not go to sea. They only travel on rivers, lakes, and **canals**. Wide, flat **barges** carry **cargo** along rivers.

Large barges are often seen on many of the world's rivers.

Fishing boats

Every day, people go out to sea in their fishing boats to try to catch fish. Some fishing boats stay at sea for many days. Some even stay at sea for weeks.

These people are sorting the fish that have been caught.

net

The nets on a fishing boat are kept
tidy when the fishing is done.

Large nets are used to catch the fish. The people
throw the nets into the sea. The boat pulls the
nets along behind it and traps the fish.

13

Gondolas

In Venice in Italy, there are **canals** instead of streets. People use boats called gondolas on the canals. Gondolas are used as water taxis to get around the city.

canal

Gondolas are a nice way to see the sights of a city.

Gondoliers use the pole to balance as well as steer.

The person who sails a gondola is called a gondolier. The gondolier stands in the boat. A very long pole is used to move and **steer** the gondola.

Ferries

A ferry is a ship that carries cars, trucks, buses, and passengers. The vehicles are parked on **decks** inside the ship. Passengers sit on the upper decks.

upper deck

B.C. FERRIES

SPIRIT OF VANCOUVER ISLAND

Some ferries are so large that they have cafés and shops on board.

bow

ramp

Cars drive on to the lower decks of a ferry.

There is a huge door in the ferry's **bow**. It opens to let vehicles drive on and off. This type of ferry is called a roll-on, roll-off ferry.

Hydrofoils

passengers

The shape of a hydrofoil helps it to move at high speeds.

A hydrofoil is a very fast type of boat. It is often used to carry passengers. Hydrofoils zoom along with their **hulls** out of the water.

On the bottom of the hydrofoil's hull are small wings. These are called foils. As the hydrofoil speeds up, the foils lift it out of the water.

Aircraft carriers

An aircraft carrier has a runway along one of its sides.

runway

An aircraft carrier is a type of ship used by a navy. It is like an airfield at sea. Planes can take off and land on its huge **deck**.

A catapult gives planes a push so they can go fast enough to take off. When the planes land, they are stopped by a strong wire stretched across the deck.

It takes great skill to land a plane on an aircraft carrier.

Sailing

A junk is a sailing ship used in China for moving **cargo**. When the wind blows, it pushes on the sails. This makes the junk move along.

Junks today looks the same way they would have looked two thousand years ago.

sail

mast

bamboo pole

Bamboo is very strong, so a junk can sail in strong winds.

A junk's sails are made of cloth. Bamboo poles sewn to the sails make them stiff. Tall, wooden posts called masts hold up the sails.

Container ships

Containers are metal boxes that are filled with different sorts of goods or **cargo**. A container ship carries hundreds of containers in its **hold** and on its **deck**.

containers

hold

Most cargo travels across oceans in container ships.

crane

containers

The size and shape of containers means they can all stack easily.

The containers are all the same size. They arrive at a **port** on trucks and railway wagons. Huge cranes load the containers on to the ship.

Power boats

A power boat is a small, fast boat used for racing. Power boats have very powerful **engines**. They skim across the surface of the water.

Power boats travel so fast that their **bow** barely touches the water.

Driving a power boat is like driving a racing car.

When the sea is rough a power boat jumps from wave to wave. The **crew** have a very bumpy ride. They must wear seat belts and crash helmets to stay safe.

Cruise liners

A cruise liner is a holiday ship. On the ship there are restaurants, shops, swimming pools, and rooms for passengers. The rooms are called cabins.

A large cruise liner can carry more than a thousand passengers.

life jackets

lifeboat

Passengers put on life jackets when they get into a lifeboat.

A cruise liner carries small boats called lifeboats. In an emergency the passengers and **crew** climb into the lifeboats. Then the lifeboats are lowered safely into the sea.

Timeline

3500 BCE   The Ancient Egyptians build sailing ships with square sails and oars. They are the first sailing ships that we know about.

1000 CE   The Viking people of Northern Europe build strong wooden longboats.

1519   The Portuguese explorer Ferdinand Magellan and **crew** set out from Europe. One of his ships sails completely around the world.

1620   Dutchman Cornelis Drebbel builds the world's first submarine.

1808   A boat called the *Clermont* carries passengers along rivers in the United States. It is the first boat powered by a steam engine.

1912   The passenger liner *Titanic* sinks after hitting an iceberg in the Atlantic Ocean. More than 1,500 people die.

2006   The largest cruise liner in the world, the *Freedom of the Seas*, is launched. There is an ice skating rink, a rock climbing wall, and a surfing pool with a wave machine on this ship.

Glossary

barge	long, flat boat
bow	front of a boat or ship
canal	deep, wide ditch filled with water that boats and ships can sail along
cargo	goods carried on a ship
crew	people who work on the boat or ship
deck	flat floor on the top of or inside a boat
engine	machine that powers movement using fuel. A ship's engine moves the ship along.
hold	part of the ship where cargo is stored
hull	main part of a boat or ship. The hull sits in the water.
port	place on the coast or on a large river where ships go to load and unload their cargo
propeller	part of the boat that spins round and moves the boat forward
rudder	part of the boat that is used to steer
steer	guide the direction of the boat or ship
stern	back of a boat or ship

Find Out More

Getting Around by Boat, Cassie Mayer (Heinemann Library, 2006).

Go Facts ... Transport: Boats, Ian Rohr (A & C Black, 2005).

Wheels, Wings and Water: Boats, Lola Schaefer (Raintree, 2003).

Wild About Boats, Steve Parker (Ticktock, 2003).

Index